Other books by Binkey Kok Publications

Eva Rudy Jansen
Singing Bowls
A Practical Handbook of Instruction and Use
ISBN 90-74597-01-7

Eva Rudy Jansen
The Book of Buddhas
Ritual Symbolism Used
on Buddhist Statuary and Ritual Objects
ISBN 90-74597-02-5

Eva Rudy Jansen
The Book of Hindu Imagery
The Gods and their Symbols
ISBN 90-74597-07-6 PBK
ISBN 90-74597-10-6 CLOTH

Dirk Schellberg
Didgeridoo
Ritual Origins and Playing Techniques
ISBN 90-74597-13-0

George Hulskramer
The Life of Buddha
From Prince Siddhartha to Buddha
ISBN 90-74597-17-3

Töm Klöwer
The Joy of Drumming
Drums and Percussion Instruments from around the World
ISBN 90-74597-13-9

THE COMPLETE BOOK OF CHINESE HEALTH BALLS

THE COMPLETE BOOK OF CHINESE HEALTH BALLS

BACKGROUND AND USE OF THE HEALTH BALLS

by

AB WILLIAMS

Binkey Kok Publications bv, Havelte, Holland

First Published in 1997 by
Binkey Kok Publications bv
Hofstede "De Weide Hoek"
Meenteweg 2-3, Havelte 7971 RZ
The Netherlands
Fax: 31 521 591925

CIP-DATA KONINKLIJKE BIBLIOTHEEK, DEN HAAG

Williams, Ab
    The Complete Book of Chinese Health Balls / Ab Williams
    [transl. from the German by Tony Langam ... et al. ;
    photo's Eelco Boeijnga; ill. Inez Woldman]. – Diever ;
    Binkey Kok. – Ill., photo's
    Transl. of: Het complete Meridiaankogelboek – Diever Holland,
    Binkey Kok, 1996.
    ISBN 90-74597-28-9
    Subject headings: Chinese Health Balls / Alternative Medicine.

Lay-out: Eva Rudy Jansen
Cover design: Jaap Koning.

Typeset in 11 point Times

Printed and bound in the Netherlands.
01 00 99
10 9 8 7 6 5 4 3

Table of Contents

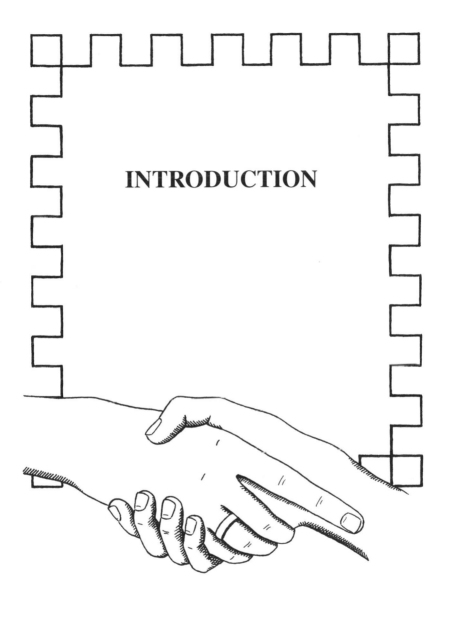

INTRODUCTION

Introduction

Chinese Health Balls are easy to use, and don't require any physical prowess. You can buy the balls in many health food stores, in gift shops, or get a friend to give you a pair. Children can use them to develop motor skills and discipline; older people can use them to promote and maintain the functioning of the vital organs. Young people will find that the mesmerizing motion of the Health Balls quickly and naturally brings them into a meditative state, where the mind is emptied of daily hassles.

Long before written language was developed, during the process of pushing back the wilderness, we learned to use tools, fire, and domestic animals to ensure that we had enough food to eat and safe shelter for the night. When the days were no longer fully taken up with meeting the most basic requirements of life, we gained free time to develop a taste for the pleasant things in life. The world of crafts, the use of spears, hammers, and bellows was a determining factor in this. But at the same time, we also developed other ways of using our hands, where the results were no longer tangible products, but were expressions of beauty, devotion, nurturance, community, and the inner life of the human individual. This work with the hands, in all its forms, produces satisfaction and a sense of self-fulfillment. Hands play a central role in civilization; they speak an international language and say everything about a person.

Hands are important for play; hands are also important in the esoteric arts and spiritual life. Many games, now usually played only by children, are actually the remnants of religious rituals that go back to the dawn of our civilization. Other games undoubtably developed so that young people could practice and perfect certain skills.

To the uninitiated observer, the use of the Chinese Health Balls may seem like a "mindless game." It is our aim, with this book, to keep Chinese Health Balls from being relegated to such a classification. Many games have deeper significances that have been forgotten over the passing of time. Their origins lie within religious activities that have been lost over the years. The following games, in which the hands have a decisive role, are still played today all over the world.

Dice
Since time immemorial, great powers have been ascribed to the hair, teeth, and bones of both animals and humans, and the rod, chair, and stone were believed to play a mysterious role in augury. Throughout the course of history, people often consulted the Fates when difficult decisions had to be made. For example, people threw knuckle bones or cowrie shells, or cast dice to ask the advice of the gods. The roots of the "modern" variations go back about 5000 years. It is crystal clear that casting dice originated from magical activity. [1]

String Games
Many variations are played throughout the world. It is possible to create amusing and complicated figures—"Cat's Cradle" and "Jacob's Ladder," for example—with a piece of string and the dexterous use of your hands. A mysterious and interesting fact is that people from completely different cultures produce string figures that are totally identical!

Bocce
The writings of an Ancient Greek physician described a certain type of game played particularly by older men. This must have been a precursor of the French game of "jeu de boules," which Italian men now play all over the world. It's very healthy!

Mikado (Pick Up Sticks)
This game is said to have its origins in China, and it requires patience, concentration, and a steady hand. Originally, valuable, carved pieces of ivory were used, which were later replaced by gaily colored wood-

---

[1]   For a full exploration of the magical origins of dice and games in general, see Nigel Pennick, *Secret Games of the Gods* (York Beach: Samuel Weiser, 1989).

en sticks. The sticks are bunched together in the hand, and then let go above a table or the floor so that they fall and spread out randomly. The aim is to pick up each stick, one at a time, without moving the others.

Marbles
This game goes back further than our nostalgic memories. It was played in Ancient Egypt and in pre-Christian Rome, and is still played in every schoolyard.

Prayer Beads
Apart from being enjoyable, games also serve as a preparation for the creative process and for practicing manual skills. In an esoteric and spiritual respect, the use of the hands, from large gestures to the smallest movement of the hand or finger, can often have a great magical effect. Gradually, exercises developed alongside this magical activity to enhance a sense of tranquillity, meditation, and concentration, either with or without the use of objects. You have to see the magical finger language (mudras) of a Zen Buddhist monk to experience what the symbolism of the fingers can add to meditation.

In the daily life of believers, the hands play an important role. The sign of the cross, the folded hands, the cross made on children's forehead before they go to sleep, your hands covering your face during meditation, are all part of religious ritual.

We find virtually identical forms of meditation in completely different civilizations. For example, in the Roman Catholic Church, the rose, as the queen of flowers, became the symbol of the Virgin Mary, and of exalted virginity, which resulted in the use of the rosary. These prayer beads, consisting of 15 large and 150 small beads, are used for repeatedly saying several prayers.

The Islamic rosary—the Misbaha ("the object for honoring")—consists of 33 or 99 beads. Practicing Muslims will rarely let it out of their hands, and use the Misbaha to pronounce the "99 most beautiful names of God." Nowadays, a devout proverb is often spoken when touching a bead. The Turkish name for this rosary is Tespih.

Rosaries are also widely used in China and Japan, and are also used by Tibetan Buddhists. It is generally assumed that they were first used by Hindus. Buddhists use the malas, prayer beads consisting of 108 beads. They are characteristic of the Northern or

Mahayana school, with its belief in the usefulness of meditation and the repetition of mystical activities. A Mantra is spoken for every bead. Two separately knotted strands serve to count the number of "rounds."

Buddhists often do between five and twenty cycles a day. One Buddhist monk once told us that he estimated he had done more than two million cycles. It is not uncommon for malas to be used so much that their round shape is worn down to an oval.

When Chinese Health Balls were used in ancient China, it was discovered that exercising with the health balls as part of meditation could also be helpful in achieving a physical and spiritual balance— a healthy life.

CHINESE HEALTH AND CHINESE PHILOSOPHY

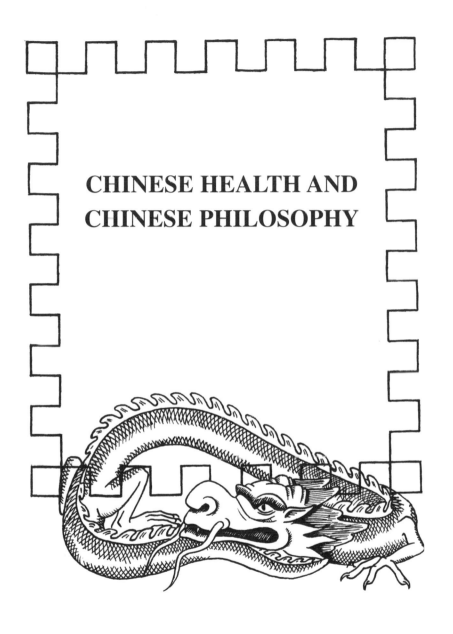

Chinese Health Balls and Chinese Philosophy

Taoism

In order to fully understand how to use Chinese Health Balls, it is necessary to look at some basics of Eastern philosophy. Taoism comes from the word Tao, which simply means "the balanced or harmonious Path." The path, and the person who is following it, are essentially one. There is a saying in Taoism that states: if the wise person does not emanate wisdom and the holy man does not emanate goodness, they can both save themselves the trouble of teaching!

The fundamental aim of the Taoist is to achieve a balance between Yin and Yang, the two Great Forces, the two poles between which everything takes place.All living creatures are part of nature and therefore of Yin and Yang. A paradox, commonly used to explain things in Taoism, is: simplicity is necessary in relating to the complexity of human nature and the self. To put it more concisely, simplicity is exceptionally complicated.

Traditional Taoism, the most intellectual of all the world philosophies, considers every aspect of the human in its totality: the mental, emotional, and spiritual aspects. In Taoism, the senses do not play a very important role. They are the instruments of a fundamental dynamic force, and they merely give access to limited sorts of circumstances. The senses are only a very small part of the total being, and are neither sought nor denied, although they are accepted as a natural part of being human. The experiences that the senses produce result in the development of subjectivity. Just as it is impossible to gain an insight into the quality of the water of a whole river by taking a water sample in one place, it is not possible to realize an encompassing view of things through the senses.

The Taoist aim is achieve a balance within is similar to the balance sought by people working with Chinese Health Balls. You can only achieve balance around you when you are able to create balance in yourself.

Yin and Yang

Yin and Yang, the Two Great Forces, form the primal substance in which Yin represents the physical, emotional, intuitive, slow qualities (the square), and Yang represents the intellectual, energetic, spiritual qualities (the circle). Yin and Yang are, respectively, the passive and the active element, the restrained and the productive aspects, which are kept in balance by the flow of energy.

The energy of the eternal interaction between Yin and Yang is called "Qi." Qi (or Ch'i, or Ki) is the energy of life, the force that moves, guides, and controls everything. Without Qi, there is no life, but without life, there is no Qi. Qi is the primal force from which everything is created and will constantly be recreated. When you work with Chinese Health Balls, you affect the balance of Yin and Yang within yourself so that Qi can flow more freely throughout your body. We'll explain how this is done through stimulating reflexology zones and the meridians—the channels for the flow of Qi—in later sections on acupuncture, acupressure, and reflexology.

It is not accurate to translate Yin and Yang as the female and male principles; it is better to speak of the passive and the active principle, the receptive and the productive aspects. Obviously, these relate to the male and female elements, but they are merely one aspect among many others. Yin and Yang are indivisible elements of a whole, and that which is indivisible can only maintain itself in relation to something else.

It is our task to find balance, and this balance is achieved by seeing the extremes—the opposite poles—and understanding their significance. Opposites cannot exist without their counterpart.

The first idea of complementary opposites was probably that of Great Mother Earth, as opposed to Father Heaven. Father Heaven controls the sun, thunder, lightning and the rain essential for growth and ripening—fertility and life—of Mother Earth.

As with light and darkness, these counterparts complement each other and work together, but at the same time they can exclude and even destroy each other. Thus opposite poles are always connected, and at the same time they conflict with each other. A balance is maintained when we understand how to manage both energies.

There is an endless series of opposite poles—Sun and Moon, male and female, spiritual and physical, attractive and repellant, dynamic and static—but there is no true opposition in the effect of these forces. Each contains an element of the other. This principle is clearly illustrated in the symbol for Yin and Yang (see figure 1): within the circle is a light comet-like shape above a dark one, and within each is a dot the color of its opposite.

In a balanced person, the body, spirit, emotions, and intellectual qualities interact harmoniously—there is a balanced interaction of Yin and Yang. However, most things, lioe water and fire, can be both good and evil. For example, Samaritans use their energy to help others, while thieves use the same energy to steal. Yin and Yang, in and of themselves, are neither good nor evil—it is when they are out of balance that apparantly negative circumstances arise.

The body is a mechanism that is constantly adapting to its environment, ensuring that the biological conditions of existence in the world are met. The expression "multiplicity in unity" indicates that no part of the body can function without the others. In Chinese phi-

Figure 1. Yin and Yang.

losophy, health is seen in terms of "wholeness," and sickness means a lack or a failure in a link in this wholeness. Westerners have tended to focus on a single cause or event when they try to affect change. Great energy is focused on "the problem," which can result in weakening another area because of the radical application of energy to one area. But in Eastern philosophy, the whole picture is always kept in view; gradual change, where Yin and Yang are gently brought into dynamic equanimity, brings enduring benefits.

When you are working with Chinese Health Balls, you may not notice any radical changes because the exercise gently effects all areas of the body at once. Regular practice is a wonderful way to bring Yin and Yang into balance in your body. It's fun, too!

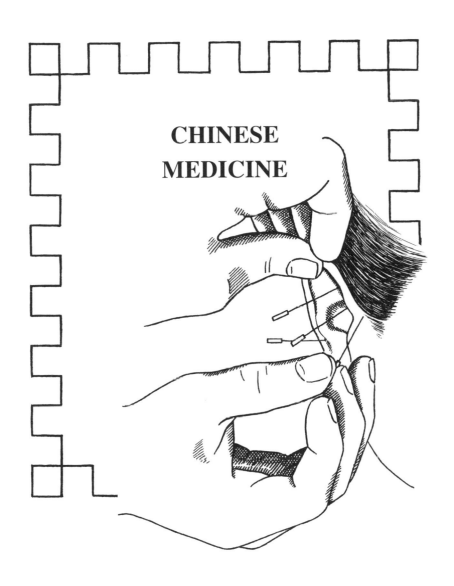

CHINESE
MEDICINE

Chinese Medicine

Chinese medicine is not the science we know in the Western world. It is based on a pre-scientific tradition. The ideas are different from those in our Western world because of the great influence of Yin and Yang in Chinese culture. Western people tend to look for a cause or something to blame. In Chinese medicine, the concepts of isolated causes and effects do not play a prominent role in diagnosis. According to Chinese philosophy, everything happens as the result of a spontaneous interaction—an inner force in the nature of things— and this also applies to medicine.

In Chinese medicine, there are four sorts of imbalance between Yin and Yang that must be considered in treatment: a shortage of Yin, a shortage of Yang, a surfeit of Yang, and a surfeit of Yin. Each of these requires a completely different treatment. Yin (the shady side of the hill) is related to qualities such as cold, quiet, passivity, the inner aspect, and darkness. Yang (the sunny side of the hill), represents qualities such as heat, movement, activity, the outer aspect, and light.

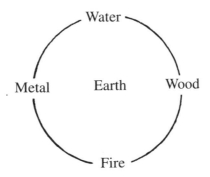

Figure 2. The Five Elements

The Theory of the Five Elements is also a part of medical therapy. The elements are Metal, Water, Wood, Fire, and Earth (see figure 2 on page 23). If one of these elements is out of balance, this will result in a degree of imbalance in the Qi of the body, soul, or spirit. Obviously, the extent to which the balance is disrupted determines the seriousness of the sickness.

Every element belongs to a particular season: Water with Winter, Wood with Spring, Fire with Summer, Earth with late Summer and Metal with Autumn. Wood and Fire are predominantly Yang, Metal and Water predominantly Yin, while Earth indicates the period balanced between the active (Yang) and the resting (Yin) phase. Traditional Chinese medicine has developed five principles related to Yin and Yang: [2]

- Everything has two sides, a Yin side and a Yang side. The front of the body is viewed as being Yin, the back as Yang. Additionally, the right side of the body is considered primarily Yang, while the left side is primarily Yin.
- Every aspect of Yin and Yang can again be subdivided into Yin and Yang. Diseases which are characterized by heat, strength, and hyperactivity are Yang, while diseases characterized by weakness, cold, and lack of activity are Yin. However, a Yin disease may reveal Yang aspects.
- Yin and Yang create each other. For example, it is not possible to refer to temperature without mentioning the Yin and Yang aspects of cold and warm. In a disease, hyperactivity is significant only in relation to passivity.
- Yin and Yang regulate each other. If there is a surfeit of Yin, there is not enough Yang, and vice versa. A disease with "fire in the body" can be caused by too little water.
- Yin and Yang merge together. There are two sorts of changes: harmonious and sudden changes. A harmonious change in disease is characterized by the gradual restoration of balance by treatment. A high fever (Yang) contains the danger of sudden shock (Yin). Finally, when Yin and Yang divide, this is the end of existence; the patient has died.

---

[2] See Manfred Porkert, *The Theoretical Foundations of Chinese Medicine Systems of Correspondence* (Cambridge and London: MIT Press, 1974).

Working with medicine is like making a painting. Everywhere in Chinese art, the artist tries to express the concepts of harmony and change that are contained in the theory of Yin and Yang. They view a painting as a microcosm of the universe. In the same way, a Chinese doctor sees a human being as a microcosm. If the characteristics are not in balance, the person is ill (the painting is ugly). Chinese medicine recognizes and requires the recognition and assessment of these characteristics so that the physician can systematically describe, diagnose, and treat diseases.

Based on this ancient tradition, Chinese medicine has been able to constantly renew itself. Every dynasty has produced important physicians. Because Chinese medicine is open to change, open to looking at changing causes and symptoms, physicians could conscientiously ask themselves what treatments were valuable, what had become unsuitable and what could be added. Therefore, despite the fact that the tradition is more than two thousand years old, Chinese medicine can be considered to be completely alive.

The Twelve Meridians

Qi (Ch'i) is that which gives us life. Chinese medicine is based on the study of Qi. In the West, this word is translated by terms such as primal force, life force, energy, vital force, but it is difficult to understand a concept that does not really exist in our Western philosophy.

Qi flows through the body along pathways which are known as meridians (see figure 3 on page 27). The Chinese discovered that each of the twelve meridians is related to a particular organ, which inherently has either a Yin or a Yang function. Via each meridian, it is possible to influence the functions of the related organ. There are many complicated theories about the specific interactions between each meridian and its related organ. The study of a patient's movements, rhythm, balance, flow of energy and change enables a doctor to arrange treatment in such a way that it results in a more harmonious state of health.

The Five Elements and the Meridians

To use Chinese Health Balls, you need a basic overview of how the elements and meridians work together. In simple terms, each of the five elements is connected to two meridians, with the exception of the Fire element, which is connected to four meridians. See figure 3 on page 27.

The element Wood: Liver (Yin) and gall bladder (Yang) meridian;
Earth: Spleen (Yin) and stomach (Yang) meridian;
Metal: Lungs (Yin) and large intestine (Yang) meridian;
Water: Kidney (Yin) and bladder (Yang) meridian;
Fire: Heart (Yin), circulation (Yin), small intestine (Yang) and body temperature (Yang) meridian, which is also refered to as the Triple Warmer or Triple Heater.

The meridians can be accessed only in places where they run just below the skin, though part of the pathway to its related organ is deep below the skin. In China, this has been done for more than 5000 years using acupuncture, the best-known example of Chinese medicine.

Before we go on to describe the effect and the use of the Chinese Health Balls, we will need to explain the general function of the nervous system. In addition, we provide a brief description of acupuncture techniques. We will also touch upon acupressure, and reflexology, which have become popular in the United States.

The Nervous System and Head's Discovery

Our nervous system consists of ten to fifteen billion nerve cells, or neurons (see figure 5 on page 30). In the last fifty years, we have made enormous strides forward in our knowledge of the central and peripheral nervous systems. Modern electronic equipment enables us to solve many of the mysteries of these system. The smallest electrical impulses can be recorded and analyzed. When we say that a neuron stimulates a muscle, we mean that the nerve fibers connected to the muscle tissue conduct a stimulus to the muscle, which then contracts. The impulse created by the muscle contraction is received by

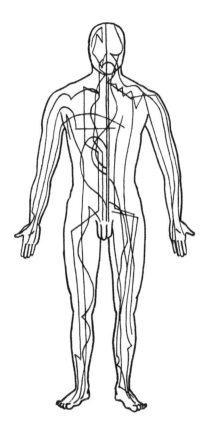

Figure 3. The Meridians.

dendrites—receptors of other neurons—and is then transported to still other neurons, or to an organ, muscle, or gland.

The synapses—the minute gaps between the dendrites of adjacent neurons—play a central role in integrating and transmitting stimuli. While the transmission of a signal is relatively simple, the activities of the neurons result in a great diversity in electro-physical effects. The reflex arc or circle is a "simple" link of nerve cells. It consists of:

1) A sensory nerve that receives the stimulus and transmits it to the central nervous system;
2) One or more connecting cells. These are the "processors" and "informers" for;

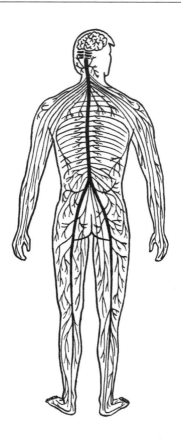

Figure 4. The nervous system.

3) The motor neuron that transmits the information from the central
   nervous system to the organ or gland concerned.

The function of the nervous system can be divided into three groups:

1) The effective integration of the activities of all the organs. The
   nervous system responds much more quickly than the circulatory
   or lymph system, and in this way ensures the functional unity of
   the individual.

2) Quick and efficient adaptation to the individual's environment.

3) Integration of the body and the spirit through special areas in the
   nervous system.

There is no room here to describe the extremely fascinating nervous
system in more detail. We want you to think about how your nervous

system, organs, glands, and muscles are interdependent. When you are working with Chinese Health Balls, you are not only exercising the muscles in your hands; you are also sending impulses throughout your entire body.

The research carried out by Head is relevant to Chinese Health Ball therapy. He discovered that every organ is connected by nerve pathways to specific areas of the skin. Disorders of an organ lead to reactions in the corresponding area of the skin. These areas of the skin are also known as the zones of Head, or dermatomes.

According to Head's theory, it is also possible to influence an organ by stimulating the relevant zone. Numerous methods of massage and therapies for treatment have been developed on the basis of Head's discovery. The massage of a certain area reduces pain and influences the organ concerned. There are also methods of treatment in natural medicine which make use of Head's theory for injections in so-called pressure points.

Long before Head's discovery, Chinese medicine was using this principle, *inter alia*, in the form of acupuncture. Where there is pain, there is an acupuncture point—the key area of the corresponding afflicted organ. There are dermatomes and acupuncture points on the hands and feet, and stimulating these areas by using Chinese Health Balls will certainly have a beneficial effect on the corresponding organs.

Acupuncture

The aim of acupuncture treatment is to restore the balance of Yin and Yang by influencing the Qi, thereby restoring health. This is accomplished by inserting very thin needles into points along the meridians. The acupuncture points have a function similar to resistors in an electrical circuit (the meridians), and inserting a needle into a point on a meridian affects the speed and force of the flow of Qi.

Archaeological studies have shown that acupuncture has been practiced for more than 5000 years. The Nei Jing, or *The Book of the*

---

[3] A translation of this was done by Ilza Veith, *Huang Ti Nei Ching Su Wen: The Yellow Emperor's Classic of Internal Medicine*, (Berkeley and Los Angeles: University of California Press, 1966).

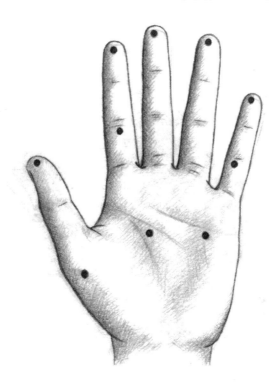

Figure 5. Acupuncture points of the hand.

Yellow Emperor, written almost 4,000 years ago, has sometimes been described as the Bible of Chinese medicine. [3] The source of all Chinese medical theories, this book resulted from hundreds of years of carefully observing and recording hypersensitivities manifested in the skin and their relationships to internal conditions of the body. The book carefully describes places—folds of skin, bony projections, hairlines or places where the structure of the skin changes—where cupuncture points are located, and the healing effect of each point is explained in detail. Acupuncture needles were once made of bronze, copper, silver, or gold. Nowadays, they are made of stainless steel and are extremely fine.

The doctor's treatment is based on a very careful observation of the changes in the patient's condition. According to the classical theory, there are 365 acupuncture points. However, in practice, a doctor uses about 150 points. It is rare for only one point to be used. Generally 5 to 15 needles are used in a single treatment. The depth to which the needle is inserted depends on the point that is chosen, and varies from 1 to 2 millimeters, in the fingertips, to 7 or 10 centimeters in the buttocks.

There are important acupuncture points on the inside of the hands (see figure 5 on page 30). In Korea, in particular, a method has been developed in which acupuncture is used only on the hands. Stimulating the points in the hand primarily affects the heart, lungs, bronchi, large and small intestine, and circulation of the blood. Using Chinese Health Balls is an excellent way to gently stimulate the points in the hand, without using needles, for the benefit of these organs and blood circulation.

Acupressure

Acupressure is based on the same theory as acupuncture. However, acupressure makes use of pressure to stimulate the meridians (see figure 6 on page 32) by massaging the acupuncture points. The massage of these acupuncture points can result in the cure or alleviation of some complaints, though proponents of acupressure do not, by any means, claim that it is a solution for all complaints.

After carefully observing the complaint or illness, a plan for the massage is drawn up on the basis of a number of fundamental rules. Then it is extremely important to take note of the reactions caused by the treatment for determining the process of further treatment. Often it is not easy to arrive at a correct diagnosis. Thus, if you have any doubt, it is advisable to consult a doctor.

Pain is the most common complaint, and can be divided into two main categories: acute pain and chronic pain. Acute pain usually results from a temporary injury or ailment, while chronic pain is associated with a longtime imbalance. There are many causes of pain, and therefore making a correct diagnosis is half the work. Following are the basic principles that need to be taken into account when applying acupressure:

• Acute pain requires only a small number of treatments (two to three), which can be given at short intervals.
• In the case of chronic pain (lasting more than fourteen days), more treatments will be needed, two to three treatments per week, and

the time between the treatments becomes longer as the healing process takes place.

- The massage should be carried out in the direction of the meridian flow if its related organ needs to be stimulated, and against the meridian flow if the organ needs to be calmed.
- The local sensitive points must be treated by exerting powerful pressure on the painful places.
- The massage should be carried out preferably with the thumb. If the massage is not unpleasant, the pressure should be increased until it does become rather unpleasant. This feeling will soon disappear.

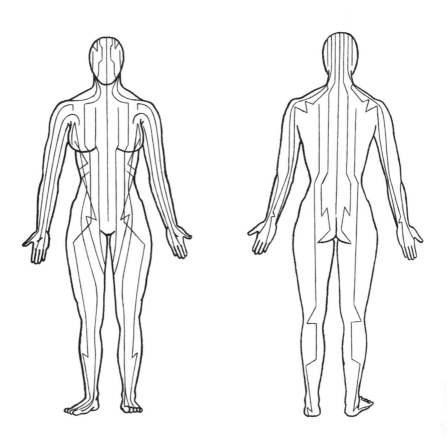

Figure 6. The acupressure meridians.

- Massage by other people is often more effective than massaging yourself, especially for areas that are difficult for you to reach yourself.

Acupressure can be helpful for treating various complaints. Obviously it may cure the complaint or alleviate the pain, but for some situations, acupressure is not appropriate. It should not be used in the following cases: if there is any abnormality or swelling where the acupressure point is located; as a treatment for cardiac patients or people with a history of heart or blood vessel disease; during pregancy or as a treatment for children under age 7; within one-half hour of a hot bath, heavy meal, or strenuous activity.[4]

Reflexology

It would be incorrect to describe reflexology as a medical therapy. Because it based on the theory of the meridians and makes use of a natural method of treatment, it is best described as a complementary way of achieving health by preventive treatment. It is a method for maintaining and stimulating the forces which keep us healthy.

It is believed that reflexology is as old as acupuncture. The American doctor, William Fitzgerald (1872-1942), studied the popular medicine of Indians, and used the massage of the hands and feet in his own practice. He came to the conclusion that the massage of certain points on the hands and feet has a positive influence on organs, alleviates pain, or even removes it altogether. He described ten zones, or meridians, five on each half of the body, which run from the skull to the sole of the feet (see figure 7 on page 34). However, it was the American doctor, Riley, who developed the method further and laid the foundations for modern reflexology with his book, *Zone Therapy*, in 1917.

The treatment makes use, above all, of your own forces. The feet are seen as a reflection of the individual. Expressions such as being "sure-footed," "having your feet firmly on the ground," and "standing on your own two feet," reflect this philosophy. We are in contact with the world around us through our feet. Thus, by massaging mainly the

---

[4] Pedro Chan, *Finger Acupressure* (New York: Random House, 1985), page 14.

feet, our own forces are activated in a simple way and we come into contact with the whole person.

Reflexology is based primarily on experience. The healing process can be stimulated by improving the flow of blood and the stimulation of the organs. Reflexology involves a careful and gentle approach to life energy. It is a therapy that is particularly suitable for healthy people who wish to remain healthy. Only a doctor, or experienced therapist, can use this massage as a supplementary therapeutic treatment.

If the same sensitive reaction repeatedly occurs in a particular area after a massage, it is a good idea to consult a doctor. However, a painful area does not necessarily mean that the organ corresponding to this zone is diseased. It could mean that massage in this area can prevent disease from developing.

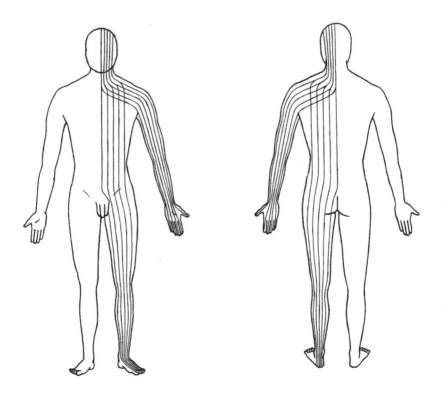

Figure 7. The Zones According to Fitzgerald.

Although reflexology has mainly developed in relation to the feet, the reflex zones of the hand are also of interest with respect to the effect of Chinese Health Balls. It is clear that the stimulation of the inside of the hands, by means of the above-mentioned principle, will also have an effect on certain organs. In general, a gentle, careful massage should release tension and result in a wonderful liberated

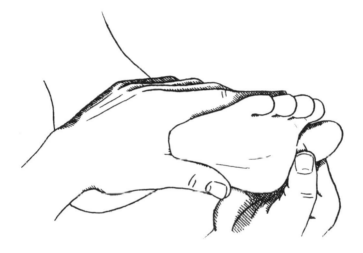

Figure 8. Foot reflexology.

feeling. A complete massage takes about an hour, and one massage per week is recommended. Reflexology is a welcome addition to a healthy life!

THE EFFECTS OF
CHINESE HEALTH BALLS

The Effect of Chinese Health Balls

According to traditional Chinese medicine, life is maintained by the effect of two forms of energy—Xue (blood) and Qi (energy, air)—which constantly interact interdependently. Like Qi, Xue has an aspect of energy in addition to its purely material aspect. However, Qi is considered to be the force or life energy that directs everything. It can be visualized as a stream of ions, or even smaller particles. Qi and Xue flow through the meridians (see figure 6 on page 32). Together with the organs that are linked to the meridians, they form the extremely complex system known in Chinese philosophy as the microcosm. The unobstructed passage of Qi and Xue in this microcosm determines a person's health.

There are three Yin and three Yang meridians running through the hand. The the heart, circulation, and lung meridians (all Yin) terminate, respectively, at the tips of the little finger, the middle finger, and the thumb. The small intestine, the Triple Warmer, and large intestine meridians commence, resepctively, at the little finger, ring finger, and index finger. These six meridians are in contact with organs and with the brain. By rotating Chinese Health Balls in the hand, many acupuncture points are stimulated, influencing the Qi in several meridians, and, consequently, in several organs.

The palm of the hand is particularly important for several reasons. The acupuncture points of the three Yin meridians are found in the palms of the hands. These three meridians are connected with the heart and lungs. The heart meridian activates consciousness and the soul, the intellect, and the memory. The heart and lung meridians are mainly responsible for the free flow of Xue and Qi. In acupuncture, Laogong, Houxi, and Shaoshang are important acupuncture points on the Yin meridians (see figure 5 on page 30). Exercising with Chinese

Health Balls stimulates these points, and can help prevent heart and lung disease, insomnia, as well as promote mental clarity, concentration, and memory.

The whole hand contains many reflex zones (see figure 9), and if these are stimulated it is possible to affect virtually all the organs. For example, the reflex zone for the neck and spinal column is at the ball of the thumb, while the on outside edge of the hand we find the zone for the shoulders and lumbar region. The area on the inside between the index finger and thumb affects the stomach, and part of the outside of the left hand, just below the little finger, affects the heart; on the right hand, this area corresponds to the liver.

In the feet there are also three Yin and three Yang meridians, which lead to various organs, and which can be stimulated by rolling the Chinese Health Balls under the feet. The liver meridian (Yin) begins at the end of the big toe; the kidney meridian (Yin) begins at the ball of the foot and circles under the arch; the spleen meridian (Yin) begins at the big toe. The bladder meridian (Yang) ends at the little toe; the gall bladder meridian (Yang) ends at the fourth toe; the stomach (Yang) meridian ends at the second toe. The most important is Zu Shao Yin, the kidney meridian. The kidneys play a central role in the urinary system. If the Yang element is insufficient, this will

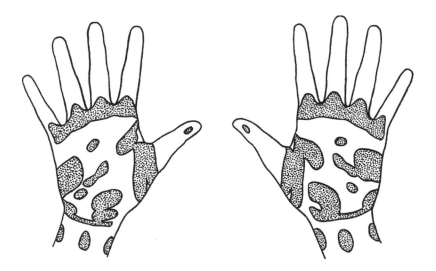

Figure 9. Reflex zones of the hand.

result in frequent urination and soft stools, while a shortage of Yin results in a tendency to dehydrate. This results in small amounts of dark urine and bouts of sweating at night.

It is possible to stimulate the meridians responsible for the liver, gall bladder, kidneys, spleen, and nose, as well as the heart and lungs, in a large number of zones on the sole of the feet (see figure 10). Experience has shown that acupuncture on the soles of the feet can be painful, while rolling Chinese Health Balls under the soles of the feet can produce the same effect without any pain, as long as this is carried out properly.

By stimulating a particular zone with Chinese Health Balls in a targeted way, anyone can positively influence all sorts of areas of the body. If you study the principles of Yin and Yang and how they flow through the meridians, and pay attention to your body's changes, you can learn how to determine the level and quality of Yin and Yang in your body. Generally, you can increase Yang energy with Chinese Health Balls by rotating them in your hand quickly so that they become warm. Or you can strengthen Yin energy by working slowly with the balls in brief sessions over an extended period of time so that the balls stay cool. In addition, the direction in which you rotate the balls affects Yin and Yang levels. Clockwise rotations will increase Yang energy, while counterclockwise rotations will increase Yin energy. Whether you are having fun, or whether you are focused on

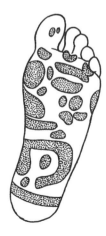

Figure 10. The reflex zones of the feet.

getting therapy with your Chinese Health Balls, regular practice will certainly improve your overall health.

To summarize:

• The twelve meridians: Qi, which gives us life (we often say energy), flows to the various organs via the meridians. The flow of Qi can be activated by the stimulation from exercising with Chinese Health Balls, activating, in particular the heart, circulation of the blood, and bronchi.

• The zones of Head: Disorders of certain organs manifest themselves in particular zones of the skin; vice versa, the stimulation of certain zones on the skin can influence the organs concerned. You can use this concept to observe changes in your body and to decide what areas need to be worked on.

• Acupuncture and acupressure use needles and pressure (massage) of Qi respectively. Treatment can result in alleviation or cure of health imbalances.

• Reflexology: The organs and areas of the body can be influenced through the ten meridians by massaging, above all, the feet, but also the hands.

But there is more !

• Practicing with Chinese Health Balls results in better circulation of the blood, and stimulates the lymph system as a result of vibration they create.

• The heat that is released when you work with Chinese Health Balls promotes circulation and also has a calming effect on the nervous system.

• Practicing with the health balls strengthens the muscles of the fingers, hands, and arms.

• The sound produced when you practice with the Health Balls has a relaxing, yet stimulating effect.

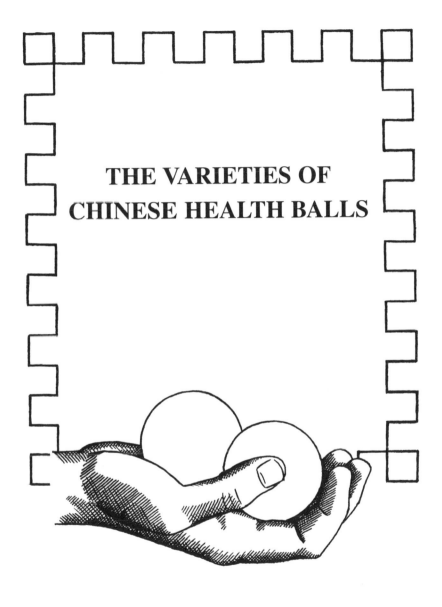

THE VARIETIES OF
CHINESE HEALTH BALLS

The Varieties of Chinese Health Balls

Chinese Health Balls are known by several different names: Baoding Balls (the name of which refers to one of the factories where these balls are made), Qi Gong ("working with energy") Balls, and Meridian Balls. In China they are referred to as *Bao Djian Tshou*, which means "health balls," or *Baici*, which translates roughly as "valuable ball." Chinese Health Balls are sold in pairs, and can be found in three basic materials: wood, stone, and metal.

No doubt, you might be confused about which type you should buy. If your intent for using Chinese Health Balls is primarily therapeutic, the metal balls are the most suitable choice. Some of these chime when they move, and while many people like this feature, if you are sensitive to sound, consider whether or not you want to hear this chiming while you practice. The metal and cloisonné balls that are commonly found in shops also have different designs, which may influence your choice.

The size and weight of the balls play an important role in choosing the right set of health balls. Generally, the larger and heavier they are, the stronger the effect on the acupuncture points and reflex zones. However, it is advisable to start with small balls. As you become more comfortable with using them, you can get a larger size, and even practice with three or four balls at a time (see pages 67-69 for exercises with three and four balls).

Any set of Chinese Health Balls makes a beautiful gift, as each pair is sold in a silk brocade box, and the materials from which the balls are made are pleasing to both the hand and eye. We'll describe each of the varieties to help you with your choice.

Wooden Balls

Wooden balls are made of hardwood, such as date palm or peach, and because of their exclusive character, they have a place in a connoisseur's collection. They are not very suitable for exercise because they are so light, but they are valued as gifts symbolizing health.

Stone Balls

Stone balls are usually made of marble or jade. Jade Chinese Health Balls not only have a beautiful green-veined, calming color, but they feel pleasantly cool and smooth in the hand. It takes a longer time for stone balls to become warm. These health balls are good to work with if you're inclined to have an excess of Yang energy in your body. The combination of the coolness of stone balls, and the tendency to handle these carefully and slowly (because of their relative fragility) contributes to soothing Yang energy. In China, jade is a symbol of purity. Jade Chinese Health Balls are highly coveted both by practitioners and by collectors. Jade Chinese Health Balls have an average weight of 300 grams and a diameter of 40 to 55 millimeters. (see figure 16).

Metal Balls

Chinese Health Balls cast in iron or turned in steel are the most widely-known and popular for several reasons. They are easy to mass-produce with high quality, they are durable, and because they are relatively heavy, they provide considerable stimulation of the acupuncture points in the hand. They rotate easily in the hand; this creates an electrostatic charge, which also effects the acupuncture points. While some metal Chinese Health Balls are solid, many are hollow and contain a spring and a second smaller ball inside, so that they chime harmoniously when rotated. The chiming helps you concentrate on smoothing the rhythm of the rotations, and many people find it to be very pleasant and soothing.

Engraved metal balls (figure 11) are also commonly used. With a phoenix on the Yin ball and a dragon on the Yang ball, they symbolize harmony, health and happiness, especially when presented as a wedding gift.

Metal balls are made in 5 sizes: 55 millimeter diameter, weighing 530 grams; 50 millimeter diameter, weighing 430 grams; 45 millimeter diameter, weighing 330 grams; 40 millimeter diameter, weighing 250 grams; 35 millimeter diameter, weighing 200 grams. (see figure 18).

Magnetic Balls

Some balls are made with small magnets on the surface. In addition to the usual effect, they also have an added effect similar to magnetic bracelets, which work on the electrostatic polarity of your body. Magnetic balls are available in two sizes: 47 millimeters, weighing 380 grams or 43 millimeters, weighing 280 grams.

The Sounding Ball

The sounding ball is a small ball with a diameter of 19 to 35 millimeters. It produces a sound composed of 28 tones that have a harmonious effect on both body and soul. Sounding balls are made of gold or silver, and are sold individually, rather than in pairs. They are often worn on a chain around the neck. True sounding balls are not really Chinese Health Balls, as their effect is predominantly based on the sound, and the weight of this ball is too slight to influence the meridians.

Balls for Children

With a diameter of only about 3.5 centimeters. and a weight of about 200 grams, these are specially adapted for a small child's hand.

Varieties of Design

Some balls are distinguished by their special appearance:

- Gold and silver balls: Gold is associated with Yin, silver with Yang.
- Black balls: These have a magnificent, dull anthracite color.
- Varnished balls: The surface is artistically painted and varnished.
- Enamel, or cloisonné, balls: These always make a sound, and are the most popular. They are magnificently decorated, often with the Yin/Yang symbol, or with a phoenix or a dragon. They have a warm, velvety feel, and the images enhance the meditational aspect of your practice.

Figure 11. Engraved Health Balls.

Figure 12. Phoenix and Dragon Cloisonné.

Figure 13. Striped Agate.

Figure 14. Yin and Yang.

Figure 15. Phoenix & Dragon Cloisonné.

Figure 16. Jade.

Figure 17. All Health Balls are sold in luxurious, silk brocade boxes.

Figure 18. Metal balls from 3.5 to 5.5 grams.

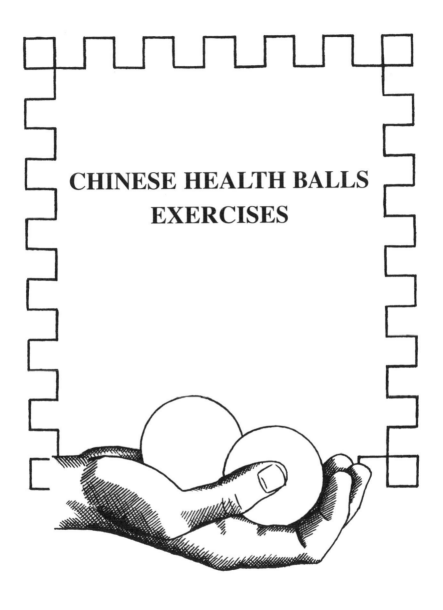

CHINESE HEALTH BALLS
EXERCISES

Chinese Health Balls Exercises

Beginning Your Practice

Despite our attempts to familiarize you with Chinese medicine and philosophy, using Chinese Health Balls will be rather strange and awkward at first. But don't get discouraged! We will describe some exercises to help you get comfortable and help you integrate your Chinese Health Balls practice into your lifestyle.

To start with, it is a good idea not to use balls that are too large for your hand. Moreover, it is best to choose a safe place to practice, because there is a chance that you could drop the balls and damage them or the floor or objects around you. Practice above an area that is well-padded with something soft and yielding.

Take your time to get used to the balls, and make sure you're in a comfortable position when you practice. It doesn't matter whether you are sitting, standing, or reclining, as long as you're comfortable. It's also good to walk while you practice, but wait until you have mastered the technique to some extent!

Warming Up
It's a good idea to start by warming up your hands. Some ways of doing this are:

• Make a fist—with your thumb outside of your palm—and then stretch open your hand as far as possible. Repeat this several times with each hand.

- Interlace your fingers and then bend your wrists away from your body so that the tips of your fingers are pressed firmly against the back of your hands; repeat this.
- Make a fist keeping your thumb under your fingers. Stretch your hand, and then make another fist. Repeat this with each hand.
- With your hand slightly open, touch the tip of all your fingers with your thumb, moving from left to right, then from right to left; then repeat this.
- Fold your hands. Stretch your thumbs. Rub your thumbs together—including the balls of the thumbs—while keeping your hands folded.

Exercises for Getting Used to the Balls

These warm-up exercises should be carried out with each hand. Try to do the exercises as rhythmically as possible. Make sure that you do them over a soft surface—on a bed or on the lawn, for example. When you start out practicing the exercises described here, it is important not to spend too much time on them. The hands and their delicate networks of muscles have to get used to unfamiliar exercise, and if you are too intense about "getting it," this can result in muscular tension, pain, or even cramping. Try to limit yourself to between five and ten minutes a day, or stop as soon as you feel any muscle fatigue. Making patient and gradual progress is usually a good way to ensure lasting success with a new activity.

- Rotate one ball in the palm of you hand by making a slight shaking/rotating movement with your wrist and arm. Your hand should be slightly cupped. Your thumb and little finger make sure that the ball cannot fall out of this cup.
- Open up your hand. "Balance" the ball from the palm of the hand to the fingertips. Try to move the ball as far up the fingertips as possible without dropping it.
- Try to rotate the ball with the tips of your fingers.
- Open your hand. Place a ball in the palm of your hand. Move the ball with your thumb to the base of your little finger and then to the base of all your other fingers. After you reach your index finger, allow the ball to roll back into the palm of the hand.

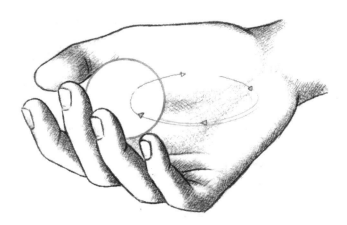

- Make a cup out of your hands, with your fingertips touching. Roll one or two balls from your left to your right hand by making a slight tilting movement.
- Toss a ball up in the air (not too high) and catch it.
- Grasp a ball, open your hand, and at the same time throw the ball up a few centimeters. Then try to rotate the ball by moving your fingers and wrist at the same time.
- Take the ball into your hand and your the hand facing down. Open your hand so that the ball drops, but then grab it as quickly as possible. This exercise can be done with a larger ball, for example, a ball from a game of *jeu de boules*, bocce, or billiards.

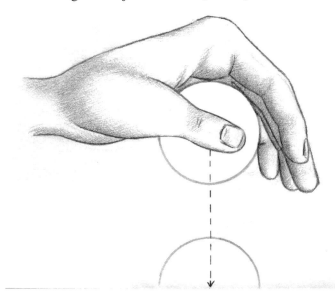

- Pick up the ball with your thumb and fingertips, so that the back of your hand is facing down. Let go of the ball, and then grab it with the whole hand as quickly as possible.
- Variation: take hold of a ball alternately with your thumb and index finger, then with your thumb and middle finger, your thumb and ring finger, and finally with your thumb and little finger.
- Variations: one ball in each hand, at the same time or alternately.
- Throw the ball from your left to your right hand and back again.
- Try doing the previous exercises without looking.
- Hold two balls firmly in one hand with the back of your hand facing down. The palm of your hand and your fingers form a hollow in which the balls can move in only one direction. With your thumb, push the ball closest to it toward your little finger, then bring it back in toward the thumb while the thumb and index finger of your free hand take hold of the ball closest to the little finger. The idea is to get used to the feeling of one ball rolling across the base of your fingers and sliding around the other. Repeat this exercise.

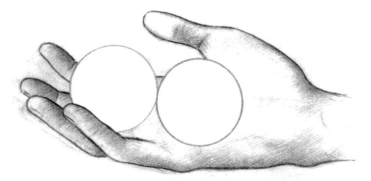

- Let two balls jump over each other. To start, use your arm to carry out the movement, but then try to perform the exercise with a swift, curving movement of your ring, middle, and index fingers.

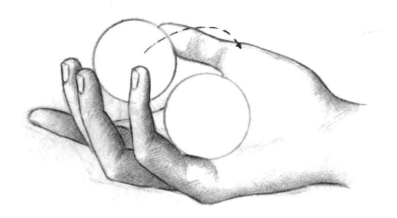

- Variation: Do a different exercise with each hand.
- To strengthen the muscles of the hand: take a ball between the tips of your five fingers, squeeze, and relax. Or leave the ball in the palm of your hand and press down on it with one finger at a time, relaxing in between each finger press.

The Basic Exercise

Rotating the two balls in the palm of your hand is the basic way to use Chinese Health Balls. Following are two methods—the total movement, and step by step—to get those balls rolling!

The Total Movement

Place two balls in the palm of your left hand. Your hand should be open and relaxed. With your thumb, index finger, and middle finger of the "free" hand, rotate the balls around each other in a counter-clockwise movement. After a while, try to support the movement with your thumb and fingers (especially the little finger) of the left hand wherever possible.

Eventually this exercise should be carried out without the support of the other hand.

When you do the exercise with the right hand, rotate the balls in a clockwise direction.

Step by Step

1. Place the balls in the hand you find easiest to use. In the following step-by-step instructions, we are refering to the right hand.

2. Open your hand so that one ball (1) is exactly in the middle of the palm of your hand, and the other ball (2) is above it on your fingers (especially the index and middle fingers). Your fingers should be slightly curved, with the tips of your fingers pointing up, and there should be minimum tension in your hand. It's also best not to have your hand resting on anything. Although it's tempting to rest your arm or hand on something, this would inhibit the motion of your fingers and arm muscles, ultimately making the exercise more difficult.

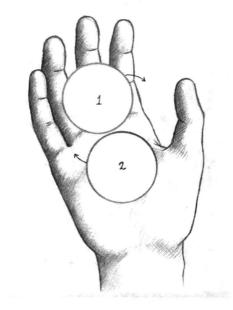

3. By exerting a slight pressure with successively your middle and index fingers, Ball 2 rolls in the direction of your thumb, and at the same time, Ball 1 is slightly displaced towards your little finger.

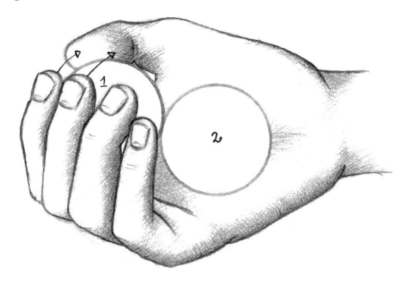

4. Increase the pressure of your thumb on Ball 2 so that Ball 1 is pressed against your little finger.

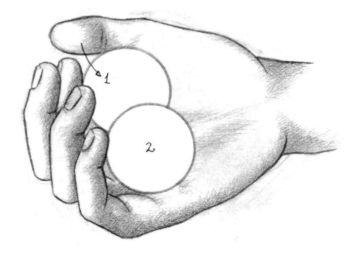

5. By pushing lightly with your little finger, middle finger, ring finger, and index finger consecutively, Ball 2 rolls toward your thumb, while at the same time, Ball 1 moves to your little finger via the ball of your thumb.

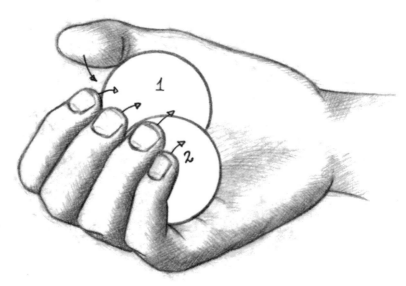

6. By exerting a slight pressure with your little finger and ring finger consecutively, the balls are returned to the starting position and the rotation is complete.

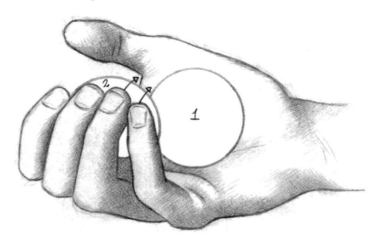

Repeat these steps until you begin to get a feel for the flowing motion, and then try them out with the other hand.

At first, the balls will audibly collide with each other, but gradually your hand will be able to rotate the balls around each other in a flowing movement, while your thumb and little finger ensure that the balls don't get off course.

The natural range of movement of the wrist makes the balls roll round more easily clockwise in the right hand and counterclockwise in the left hand. But once you have mastered the basic exercise, you can try carrying out the rotation in the opposite direction (note that we are still talking about the right hand here):

A. Make sure that in the starting position described under Point 2, your little finger is higher than your thumb.
B. Lower your ring finger and little finger slightly, and at the same time, push Ball 2 toward your little finger with your thumb, index finger and middle finger.
C. Move Ball 1 toward your thumb by lightly pushing it with your little finger.
D. Increase the pressure with your little finger, and at the same time press Ball 1 to the side with your thumb and up toward your index finger and middle finger.
E. The balls have now changed places and you can start again at B.

If you find it difficult to keep the balls in your hand, you can hold the outside of your hand against your stomach to prevent the balls from falling over the edge of your hand.

Once again, we would like to point out that at first you should not practice for too long. Make sure you're not tense; tension will not help the exercise, and can result in muscle pain and cramp.

When you're practicing with the balls, your rhythm determines the degree of harmony you achieve. Working with rhythm and harmony increases the effect of the exercise. A change in the exercise, no matter how small, also means a change in the rhythm. Rotating the balls to the left instead of the right, standing instead of sitting, working with the left hand rather than the right hand—each exercise has its own rhythm. It's important to find the best rhythm for every exercise.

After a while, you will find the basic exercise easy to perform, and you'll become aware that your general state of health improves with regular exercise. In general, for the best results, you should practice with your Chinese Health Balls for 5 to 10 minutes a day. Once you have mastered the basic exercise, you will notice that you can start to combine the exercises with other activities almost as a matter of course. You'll be able to read with a book in one hand while rotating the balls in the other; use them while watching television; do a few rotations when you get up in the morning, or before bed; practice on the bus (be careful not to drop them!) or while you're walking your dog. You could take them to your health club, and practice while you wait for your favorite equipment to be available. People will want to know: just what are those things?! Who knows—you could make some new friends with your Chinese Health Ball practice!

Aiming at the Perfect Form

If you are diligent in your practice, your hands are in good shape, and you use balls of the right size for you, you can master the basic exercise quickly. In aiming for perfection, you then have to learn to rotate the balls around each other at a regular speed so that you can hear only the soft sound of the balls rubbing together as they make contact. If you have the type of Chinese Health Balls that chime when you rotate them, you can focus on the chiming to determine the smoothness of your rhythm.

You will be able to carry out the highest form of Chinese Health Balls exercise after a good deal of regular practice. This sophisticated exercise is described below. But don't focus on this until you are virtually able to do the basic exercise in your sleep—we don't want you to get frustrated and give up! However, attempting to achieve the perfect form, and performing more difficult exercises will increase the benefit to your central nervous system as you increase your concentration and dexterity. The balls should describe the largest possible circle, and they should roll through the hand so that they don't make contact with each other.

The Starting Position

With the back of your hand pointing down, bend back your wrist as far as possible without stretching the muscles too much. Ball 1 is held between your thumb and curved index finger, while Ball 2 is pressed into youre palm with your little finger and curved ring finger. This makes the space between the balls is as large as possible.

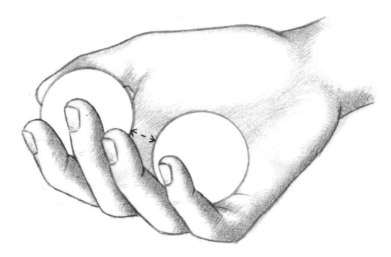

The Movements:

- Stretch your ring finger and little finger so that Ball 2 rolls down to the base of the fingers, and then hold it in place there.
- Push Ball 1 toward the base of your thumb with your curved index finger. This ball is then held between the thumb and the base of the thumb by the curved thumb.
- Straight after this movement, stretch your little finger, ring finger, middle finger and index finger consecutively so that Ball 2 rolls over the middle joints of your fingers toward your index finger. At the same time, your curved thumb pushes Ball 1 to middle of your palm.
- Ball 1 is held between the base of your thumb and your ring finger and little finger. This is done by stretching your thumb, which at the same time takes hold of Ball 2 and rolls it on to your index finger.

The second round starts by bending the index finger and slightly stretching the ring finger and little finger. As soon as you have perfected this sophisticated exercise, work on increasing the speed at which you do it. Increasing the number of rotations with a regular rhythm, and therefore with a good harmony, will increase the effect of the exercise.

Although this therapy is not meant for competitions—its importance does not lie in performance for the outside world—participants in China are known to have achieved more than two hundred rotations per minute!

Exercising with Three Balls

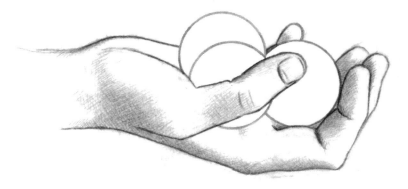

When you're ready to try the basic exercise with three balls, start with three balls of the smallest size. To prevent one of the balls from falling, keep your hand as level as possible, and spread your fingers slightly more than you would with two balls. A flowing movement requires the subtle interaction of the fingers, especially the thumb and little finger.

Your thumb always pushes Ball 1 toward your little finger, under the others. Your little finger catches the ball that is there (2) because of the pressure, and by slightly raising and curving your little finger, it pushes the Ball 2 toward your ring finger, middle finger etc., along the top. Ball 3 seems to move automatically towards your thumb. When you do the exercise with three balls, the most difficult variation is, again, to do it in the opposite direction. Here are some variations on this theme.

- With a combined movement of your ring finger, middle finger, and above all, index finger, push the top ball over the two lower balls. The ball "jumps" over the other two.

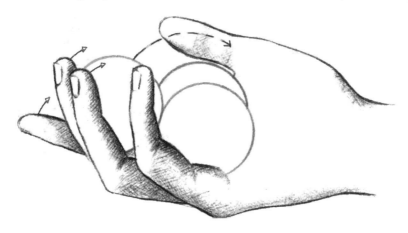

- Try the previous exercise, moving the "little finger ball" and the "thumb ball" alternately to the top position.
- You can perform combinations of the basic exercise with the exer cise described above. For example: do 5 simple rotations followed by the jump, or 3 rotations to the right, passing the little finger ball over the other two, followed by 3 rotations to the left and passing the thumb ball over the other two.
- Try keeping the little finger ball in one place, while rotating the other two balls around each other. This can be done to the right, or to the left. Repeat this exercise, but this time keep the thumb ball in its place. Perform the exercise both to the right and to the left.
- Remember to practice alternately with both the left and the right hand. You can also try to carry out these exercises with both hands at the same time. As soon as you have mastered the basic exercise in both directions, you can obviously increase the level of difficulty by using larger balls. Remember that the more difficult the exercise is, the more intense the effect will be.

Practicing with Four Balls

In order to practice with four balls, your hand must be able to control four balls, and the easiest way to do this is by choosing smaller balls. Working with four balls requires a high level of concentration as well as considerable co-ordination. All the fingers are more or less forced to co-operate. Don't be surprised if you feel like a beginner, even if you have become skilled with two or three balls. Practice makes perfect, and with the help of concentration and co-ordination, the exercise can have a great effect, especially due to the added weight of the balls.

In addition to stimulating the reflex zones of the hands more intensely, this exercise will improve your blood circulation and result in improved muscular and nervous co-ordination, especially of your hand and arm. You can also expect a beneficial effect on your entire central nervous system.

The Exercise

Choose the most comfortable, relaxed starting position, and place four balls in your hand. Tilt your hand down as far as possible, raising the side of the little finger slightly. This will prevent any of the balls from rolling out of your hand too easily. You can also use the other hand at the beginning to prevent one of the balls from dropping. You should try this exercise first with the hand that you find easiest to use. The movement is easiest to accomplish clockwise with the right hand (as described above), and counterclockwise with the left hand.

- Spread your fingers so that they are slightly curved.
- Your thumb pushes the ball that is there toward your little finger, under the other balls. The ball under your little finger is caught between it and your ring finger, as a result of the pressure exerted by your thumb.
- The ball that is in the curve of your ring finger and middle finger moves toward your index finger. The movement of the two top balls is maintained by slightly bending your little finger, ring finger, and index finger consecutively.
- The combined movement of your index finger and thumb moves the ball to your thumb by bending your index finger. It is caught,

and then pushed on without interruption toward your little finger. Now you are ready to start the second round of the movement described above.

When you have a reasonable sense of control and you are able to do the exercise with your right and left hand, it is time to start devoting attention to the meditational aspect, and/or to rotating the balls in the opposite direction as in the basic exercise.

Always remember to start by doing a warm-up exercise to prevent muscle pain or cramping, and perform these exercises in as relaxed a manner as possible.

T'ai Chi, Qi Gong and the Chinese Health Balls

Like the practice of Chinese Health Balls, T'ai Chi and Qi Gong are Chinese therapies that have a tradition of more than 2500 years. These health exercises also have a strongly preventive character.

T'ai Chi ("t'ai" means large, or great and "chi" means origin), the great origin, is seen as the mother of Yin and Yang. The health exercises are characterized by slow, flowing movements aimed at balancing the body and the spirit. As most practitioners know, regular T'ai Chi practice, which requires a fair degree of discipline, results in good health and long life.

The primary effect of T'ai Chi exercise is to prevent illness, although it can also be used to heal certain ailments. It enables patients to release tension and subsequently to work on improving their physical condition and general well being. T'ai Chi exercises increase physical strength, improve blood circulation, correct posture, improves agility, stamina, and brings relaxation to the body and spirit. T'ai Chi has a massaging effect on the joints and helps to prevent restrictions of movement caused by ailments such as arthritis or rheumatism.

The movements are controlled by the thought processes; they are slow and produce a feeling of lightness and calm. For many people who are beset by emotional problems, T'ai Chi improves their powers of concentration, self-control, and self-confidence. The benefits of T'ai Chi can be obtained by doing the exercises for 10 minutes to half an hour every day.

Qi Gong is a combination of spiritual concentration and breathing exercises. It was developed to promote and nourish the flow of energy "Qi" in the body. Qi Gong helps to cure illnesses, such as depression, high blood pressure, stomach ulcers, and inflammations. It does not involve as much movement as T'ai Chi, and is ideal for the chronically ill.

The use of Chinese Health Balls can be combined with T'ai Chi to produce a profound effect. Those who are familiar with T'ai Chi will immediately understand the combination. The energy you create with the rotations of the Chinese Health Balls can be directed, with T'ai Chi movements, throughout your body.

T'ai Chi is an extremely complicated form of physical exercise that is difficult to learn without a teacher. However, the following exercises are simple enough to give you an idea of what T'ai Chi is like, and you may want to pursue further study with a qualified instructor. Most martial arts schools offer T'ai Chi classes.

T'ai Chi Exercises—Basic Principles
Combine T'ai Chi moments with slow, natural breathing—deep, calm, regular and rhythmical. Breathing in and breathing out coincide with certain movements. Movements that go up or stretch out involve breathing in, while you breathe out during the downward movements and when you bend down or contract. Breathe from the diaphragm or stomach, which should be relaxed. Stand up straight, in a comfortable position and keep your body loose, yet controlled. Relax the muscles of the back, and let your shoulders and elbows hang down. Your limbs serve as a focus for all the movements, which are light and flowing. They should to be carried out extremely slowly, at a gentle pace. When you move your feet, mimic the way in which a cat walks, and when you move your arms, imagine that someone is pulling on them by a silk thread. Make every movement with total concentration, but with as little effort as possible. In your mind's eye, keep an image of the movements as you perform them. If you begin to feel tension, stop and loosely shake your limbs, or gently swing your arms around you, and check your breathing. Wait until everything inside you calms down, and begin again.

The Basic Stance

Figure 19. Basic stance.

Stand in a relaxed position with your head straight in line with your spinal column, your body straight, your shoulders relaxed and your arms hanging loosely at your sides. Your body should be balanced with your feet placed parallel, shoulder-width apart, and your knees slightly bent.

Focus your attention on Point A, just below the navel, as shown in figure 19 on page 72. Make sure that you are breathing in a relaxed, calm way, but with deep, regular breaths.

"Send" your breath to different parts of the body. When you breathe in, imagine that your breath is flowing in through a certain point in the body and then leaving the body at another point you have chosen. For example, imaging your breath is entering via Point A, and leaving the body from Point B. If you find it difficult to concentrate on certain parts of the body during the movements, or to redirect your breath, it is a good idea to decide on some places before your start, and begin on the easy points. For example, "breathe in" from the sole of your foot to the base of your spine, from your neck to your hands, from the ears to the hips.

Exercise 1

In the basic stance, breathe in and out in as described above for 1 or 2 minutes.

Exercise 2

Breathe in as you bring your forearms to Point C in the middle of the sternum. Hold this position for a moment, and then lower your arms back to the starting position as you breathe out. Repeat this exercise three times without forgetting the basic principles of T'ai Chi.

Exercise 3

Begin as in Exercise 2, but after reaching Point C, stretch your arms out sideways. From this position you lower the arms to the starting position, as you breathe out. Again, the exercise is carried out three times.

Exercise 4

Start as in Exercise 3, and as you stretch out your arms (breathing in), place your weight on your left leg, and extend your right leg behind you. You are now in the "bird position."

As you breathe out, return slowly and evenly to the starting position. When you repeat the exercise, stand on the right leg. Alternate between placing your weight on your left and then your right leg three times.

The exercises can be carried out separately or in succession. These are only four exercises from an enormous range of T'ai Chi forms, which have been described in numerous books by many experts. You may want to refer to the reading list we have provided for more information.

When you feel that you are able to carry out an exercise in accordance with the principles of T'ai Chi and you have become sufficiently skilled in the use of the Chinese Health Balls, you can try to combine them.

Hold two Chinese Health Balls in each hand, and during the exercises described above, try to rotate the balls in the hands. You will become aware that this is by no means easy and that some positions, such as the starting position, are not conducive to rotating the balls. Always remember that working with T'ai Chi and Chinese Health Balls is not a matter of performance or show, but some thing to practice quietly and in balance. Slowly build up your practice and avoid making any undue effort.

Excercises with the Feet

As explained in the section on Chinese medicine and the effects of Chinese Health Balls, massaging the sole of the foot stimulates many important acupuressure points and reflex zones, and therefore has many health benefits. Regular use of Chinese Health Balls with your feet will reinforce their muscles, as well as produce better co-ordination and a greater sense of balance. It can also improve the circulation of the blood in the feet and legs.

Sit down comfortably on an elevated surface so that your feet just touch the floor and your thighs are parallel to the floor. Make sure that the temperature of the floor is comfortable—after all, you are working with bare feet! Place a folded blanket or towel on the floor; this helps to add to your comfort, prevents the balls from rolling uncontrollably, and keeps away complaints from any neighbors you might have living below you, should you live in an apartment building.

Place one ball under one foot and try to master the three basic patterns: moving the ball forward; moving the ball backward; moving it in a circle (clockwise and counterclockwise). Try to carry out these exercises in a set rhythm, and after a while, try combinations of the basic patterns. Don't forget to give your other foot a turn! In this way, you are working toward practicing with both feet at the same time, carrying out combinations of exercises with good rhythm.

In addition to "treating" your whole foot, you can focus on isolating the movements under the ball of the foot and/or the heel. As the exercises become more challenging, your level of concentration will increase, and you will experience more intense effect overall.

For example, it is possible to work with two balls with each foot, and carry out the basic exercise with the hands at the same time.

Exercising Your Feet with Two Balls
Place two balls under the arch of your foot and roll them forward and backward, so that the balls remain more or less touching. If you have two sets of Chinese Health Balls, you can do this with both feet at the same time.

Place one ball under the ball of your foot and one ball under your heel, and describe small circles.

Place two balls against the inside of one foot, and massage the side of the foot using the sole of the other foot to move the balls.

In addition to the massage described above, here's an exercise to practice dexterity with the balls: Move the ball through the room to a certain place or by a certain route, moving it or pushing it like a skilled soccer player. It is important to be careful about the furniture and to avoid doing this on very smooth floors. Alternately use the inside and outside of your foot, the heel and the ball of your foot, and change feet at regular intervals.

Foot Massage and Foot Baths

An even greater effect can be obtained by combining the use of the Chinese Health Balls with a footbath. This stimulates the circulation of the blood, and brings more of the sole of your foot in contact with the water. Keep in mind that additives to the water, such as bath salts, can have a corrosive effect on the balls. Even if you use ordinary water, rinse the balls thoroughly, dry them well and rub them with a little bit of oil when you're done.

Walking Exercises

These walking exercises are most effective when you use Chinese Health Balls that chime; they improve your rhythm and increase your power of concentration.

• Hold one or two balls in each hand and allow them to sound rhythmically for each step you take.
• With each step, allow two balls in each hand to tap against each other.

- Take one ball, and as you walk, throw the ball from your left to your right hand and back. Make sure that you do this rhythmically.
- Take one ball in each hand with the back of your hand pointing up. Swing your hand forward, and at the end of the swing, let go of the ball and then catch it again. Do this rhythmically.
- When you go for a walk in a peaceful area, take two sounding balls with you. Place them against your ear so that they block the ear passage, and concentrate on the tones.
- Take two balls in each hand. Hold your arms loosely by your sides as you walk. Rotate the balls rhythmically (do the basic exercise) for every step you take.
- Perform the previous exercise, but with each step swing your arms. You can perform variations of this by swinging both arms forward at the same time, or by swinging your arms in front of your body, crossing them over each other.
- Walk slowly. Breathe in when you take the first step, and at the same time rotate the balls, as in the basic exercise, three times. Breathe out with the next step, and rotate the balls three times once again; then repeat this.

Try to carry out these exercises rhythmically and with concentration. They are clearly reminiscent of T'ai Chi.

Sound and Rhythm Exercises

Hold one ball in each hand and with rhythmical movements—shaking or rotating—try to create a melody.

The same effect can be achieved by loosely holding the ball in the palm of your hand, with your palm facing up, and tossing the ball up. It is possible to change the rhythm by holding the ball in your hand for a longer time or tossing it up higher or lower.

Make a shaking movement while firmly holding two balls in each hand. Variations of this can be created by holding the balls more loosely and allowing them to touch each other at regular intervals, or you can perform the basic exercise as you shake the balls. Another variation is to hold one ball, and toss up the other ball. In each variation, try to make sure that the exercise is done in a rhythmical way.

All the exercises described above can be done standing up or sitting down, but if you have enough space, it is also possible to accompany them with an improvised dance. Wear comfortable clothes and try to move in as relaxed a way as possible. Choose a rhythm that seems appropriate for you and listen attentively for the sounds.

Self-Massage

Take one ball in the palm of your right hand, and press it against a place on the right side of your face, keeping your hand outstretched. For example, start with your cheek. Your fingers are not used in this exercise. Exert enough pressure so that the ball stays in place. Shut your eyes, and then massage every part of the right side of your face with light, rotating movements. In this way, discover your face without leaving out any areas, taking particular care around the eyes. Change hands for the other half of your face. The next logical step is to massage the neck. Don't be alarmed if massaging the jaw and neck area leads to increased production of saliva. This massage can be carried out on every accessible part of the body.

This massage not only helps the circulation of the blood, but also stimulates the pressure points, and can relieve sinus problems. If it is carried out correctly and for an appropriate length of time, it results in a wonderful relaxed feeling. Enjoy this, take your time, and remember that after the massage a period of rest will provide good balance.

If you find that this massage is unpleasant or painful, stop and ask yourself what the reason might be. Remember that to carry out the massage, it is essential to assume a comfortable position, and be completely calm. These are preconditions for the massage to be fully effective.

Massage with a Partner

You can also have the massage carried out by a partner. Make sure that the massage environment is pleasant, and at a comfortable temperature. It's best to wear as little clothing as possible, and to do the massage after a warm shower or bath. Get in a comfortable position for the massage, and cover the parts of the body that are not being massaged with a towel or other comfortable cloth. Your partner holds a ball in each hand, and with the flat of the hand presses the ball on the area to be treated. Remember that if you have just taken a warm bath, the pressure should not be as intense as an acupressure treatment. Your partner can roll the balls in a straight line, or describe smaller or larger circles with a rotating movement. Begin the massage from the neck or the back. You lie in a relaxed position on your stomach so that your partner can treat the whole area, alternating straight lines with smaller or larger circles.

Of course, you can also have your partner massage your stomach, arms and legs. For the legs, do the massage by describing small circles from the ankles up to the groin, and then going back in straight lines. This can be repeated several times. Remember to relax after the massage.

Self-Acupressure with Chinese Health Balls

Another way some people have used Chinese Health Balls is to perform acupressure on places, such as the neck and back, that they can't reach themselves. Before you attempt this on your own, you should learn a little more about acupressure points, and you should be very careful. *The Healing Benefits of Acupressure* by F. C. Houston, P. C., is an excellent reference to use when beginning to explore acupressure points. If you have back injuries, you should check with your doctor before trying this. The basic idea is to put a pillow on the floor and position the balls on top of the pillow, and then position your body on top of the balls so that the weight of your body sends the pressure of the balls into the acupressure points. The balls should be on a soft surface so that you don't bruise yourself when you recline on them—you could place the balls on a firm bed or couch if you are uncomfortable using the floor. If you use a large enough surface, and bend your knees with your feet flat on the floor or bed, you can slowly move your body up and down to push the balls along your back.

HISTORICAL
PERSPECTIVE

Historical Perspective

The Ming Dynasty (1368 – 1644)

In the year 1368, Emperor Togan Temur was banished to Mongolia, and the impoverished land of China fell into the hands of Hong Wu (1368-1396). This was the beginning of the Ming Dynasty.

Although there are more than a thousand years between the Emperor Wu and the first emperor of the Han Dynasty, Han Gaozu (247-195 B.C.), they are often compared. They both came from the ordinary people, overthrew tyrannical regimes and established prosperous new dynasties. Both came to the throne because of their exceptional leadership qualities, combined with a native intelligence. Both dynasties were characterized by an extremely high degree of bureaucracy. Nevertheless, there were also remarkable differences, particularly in relation to the above-mentioned official hierarchy.

Han Gaozu was afraid to deviate from the unwieldy bureaucratic government that had characterized the Qin Dynasty (210 B.C.). Emperor Ming Hong Wu was in a much stronger position. He had sucessfully led the national uprising against Togan Temur, and without any rivals or political uncertainty, his authority was greater than that of any other Chinese emperor, with the possible exception of Qin Shi Huangdi (684-642 B.C.).

The prosperous middle classes were delighted that Togan Temur had been banished, because they had been very badly treated. They did not hesitate to fill the important positions in the Ming bureaucracy. It soon became clear that there was no room in the Ming Dynasty for the old established order. The Emperor ruled in person with the help of a sort of cabinet, which had a co-ordinating task. The system of bureaucracy functioned well, but for the first time it deviated strongly from Confucianism, the philosophy of harmonious life based on right conduct, restraint, and individual subjugation to social roles.

During the Ming period, the officials of the bureaucratic system acted in an increasingly individual way. When the Emperor started to withdraw behind the walls of his residence, the Forbidden City, because of the many conflicts between the highest officials, the era of the Eunuchs started. They became essential intermediaries between the official world outside and the Emperor. Every civil servant who wished to bring something to the Emperor's attention had to use the services of the Eunuchs, and it did not take them long to attain a very powerful position.

The Ming period can be described most accurately as a period of conservatism. Throughout the land, garrisons were quartered in strategic places. Military colonists were assigned land there and had to provide for their own needs. All contacts with foreigners were strictly regulated. The foreigners (barbaric people) who visited China had to send emissaries to the court. They would have to show their subjugation to the Emperor by kneeling three times and touching the ground with their forehead. They also had to bring gifts in the form of products from their own country. This so-called system of tribute, which was used in China from the Ming Dynasty onward, regularly led to difficulties in the following centuries, particularly in the contacts with Europeans.

Although trade abroad declined, probably as a result of the system of tribute, internal trade and commerce flourished. Many taxation reforms were introduced. Taxes had to be paid in silver instead of the usual products "in kind." Paper money was also abolished.

Large and small towns became extremely prosperous. China was not a country of large urban centers with impressive tall buildings. Most of the buildings were very low, and from this, outsiders might have concluded—incorrectly—that the country was not very prosperous.

The Ming Dynasty was characterized by a glittering cultural and social life. In literature, the development of the novel was quite remarkable. The *Hsi-yu-chi* by Hsuan Tsang, the notes of a pilgrimage to the West, is very famous. Another famous work is the imperial encyclopedia from the Yung-Lo period, the *Yung-Lo ta-tien*.

Originally there were 11,000 handwritten copies, but only 400 volumes of the most important works in a variety of fields have survived. Without any exaggeration, it is true to say that the plays by Tang Xianzu about family dramas and social conflicts are comparable to the most famous Western works.

Painting in the Ming Dynasty was technically of a very high standard, cultivated mainly from earlier styles. The academic painters at the court were obviously subject to strict rules and regulations.

The novels, paintings and plays evoke a picture of the life of prosperous people during the second half of the Ming Dynasty.

There were large residential complexes, walled, and with heavy doors. The homes were a delight to see. They were adorned with great detail, sparkling lacquer work, shining rosewood furniture, enamel work, and ornaments in jade and ivory.

The art of ceramics flourished. Generally, the ceramic work of the Ming period was characterized by a generally simple, robust design, and sometimes by a fairly casual finish. This is found particularly in the blue and white porcelain, the dominant ceramic work of this dynasty, which was exported to other eastern countries in large quantities. In 1602, it was exported to Holland where it became popular as "cracked" porcelain.

At the highest social and economic level, this was a very erudite society. The boys from wealthy families received a long and thorough classical education, from age 6. A national examination was taken about age 30. Those who passed these exams successfully were given lucrative jobs in the bureaucratic system and gained considerable social standing. Obviously, the art of printing contributed to the dissemination of large numbers of philosophical, technical, historical, poetic, and political works.

There was no clear distinction between life in the towns and in the countryside, and because of the enormous diversity of the Chinese countryside, there was no clear dividing line between lords and peasants. Chinese farmers worked hard, the land was fertile, and various forms of reciprocal aid in the case of natural disasters or when the countryside was threatened by hordes of bandits, contributed to several centuries of prosperity.

China had many rich Buddhist and Taoist temples, as well as temples dedicated to the forces of nature, temples for the ancestors, sacred places for Confucius, mosques and synagogues.

Wang Yang Ming's school of philosophy was very influential. Reacting to the Neo-Confucianist orthodox doctrine, Wang Yang Ming believed that knowledge should be extended by study. Each person should try to acquire an intuitive knowledge by studying his own personal *li*, or pattern of being within the universe. [5] This development of the self had the character of meditation. Individual morality became the predominant factor.

Wang Yang Ming's opponents considered his teachings as one of the causes of the decline of the Ming dynasty. This decline could also be attributed to the corruption resulting from the decay of the general moral norms and the growth of an unbridled individualism.

Chinese Health Balls in Historical Perspective

During the Ming Dynasty, Chinese Health Balls were first related to health, and therefore this period is seen as the time when Health Balls came into popularity.

The archives of the Baoding factory, in the province of Hebei, can tell us a lot about the origin of these balls. They reveal that during the Han Dynasty (A.D. 26-220), walnuts were being used to train the hands. By the time of the Sung Dynasty (960-1279), real balls were used for this purpose.

Practitioners of the martial arts demonstrated their use as a weapon and acrobats also used them to demonstrate their skills. It is said that the use of the balls gives magic powers which enhance physical performance.

Emperor Jia Jing (1522-1567) introduced the balls to his court and had their effect studied thoroughly.

There is another reason why the Chinese Health Balls are inextricably linked with the Ming Dynasty. Up to that time, solid balls had been used. Influenced by the attention devoted to the use of the balls, a method was developed for making hollow balls. The true Meridian Ball came into being.

---

[5] For an exploration of the concept of *li*, see Alan Watts, *Tao: The Watercourse Way* (New York: Pantheon Books, 1975), pages 45-55.

It is worth noting that a few centuries later, the physician of the Emperor Qianlong (1736-1799), from the Qing Dynasty, prescribed daily practice with the Chinese Health Balls for the Emperor. He was so enthusiastic about the results that he turned their use into a cultivation practice. As a result, they became widely used, and the manufacture led to the creation of true *objects d'art*. A second smaller ball and a tin spring were incorporated in the hollow ball. This meant that when the balls were rotated, they produced melodious sounds.

The material value of the balls increased significantly, and more and more people used them. Both the Emperor and his physician reached an extremely old age, which promoted the use of the Chinese Health Balls even further. Qianlong was the longest reigning Emperor in the history of China.

The magical powers of the balls were highly valued in China. They were purchased for home use and were often presented as gifts to friends or older people to symbolically wish them health or recovery from illness. Even today it is customary to rotate the balls in the hand when you go for a walk, or when you receive guests. The training with Chinese Health Balls is a valuable part of the traditional Chinese system of health care.

Suggested Reading

Chia, Mantak. *Chi Self-Massage: The Taoist Way of Rejuvenation.* Huntinton, NY: Healing Tao Books, 1986.

Fenton, Peter. *Shaolin Nei Jin Qi Gong.* York Beach, ME: Samuel Weiser, 1996.

Galante, Lawrence. *Tai Chi: The Supreme Ultimate.* York Beach, ME: Samuel Weiser, 1981.

Goodman, Saul. *The Book of Shiatsu.* Garden City, NY: Avery, 1990.

Houston, P. C., F. C. *The Healing Benefits of Acupressure: Acupuncture Without Needles.* New Canaan, CT: Keats Publishing, 1991.

Lewis, Judith and Richard Leviton. *The Complete Book of Reflexology Remedies.* Englewood Cliffs, NJ: Prentice Hall, 1996.

McNamara, Rita J. *Toward Balance: Psycho-Physical Integration and Vibrational Therapy.* York Beach, ME: Samuel Weiser, 1989.

Norman, Laura and Thomas Cowan. *Feet First: A Guide to Foot Reflexology.* New York: Simon & Schuster, 1988.

Thie, John. *Touch for Health: A New Approach to Restoring Our Natural Energies.* Marina del Ray, CA: DeVorss & Co., 1987.

Turgeon, Madeleine. *Right Brain – Left Brain Reflexology: A Self-Help Approach to Balancing Life's Energies with Color, Sound, and Pressure-Point Techniques.* Rochester, VT: Healing Arts, 1993.

Watts, Alan. *Tao: The Watercourse Way.* New York: Pantheon Books. 1975.

Williams, Tom. *Chinese Medicine: Acupuncture, Herbal Remedies, Nutrition, Qigong, and Meditation for Total Health.* Rockport, MA: Element Books, 1995.

Yang, Jwing-Ming. *Chinese Qigong Massage: General Massage.* Jamaica Plain, MA: YMAA Publication Center, 1992.
——— *The Root of Chinese Chi Kung: The Secrets of Chi Kung Training.* Jamaica Plain, MA: YMAA Publication Center, 1989.
Zhang, Fuxing. *Handbook of T'ai Chi Ch'uan Exercises.* York Beach, ME: Samuel Weiser, 1996.

Also published in this series:

Eva Rudy Jansen

Singing Bowls
A Practical Handbook of Instruction and Use

What is a singing bowl? Streams of refugees have left Tibet since the Chinese invasion, bringing with them various ritual objects now being sold in the West. This book explains the Himalayan bowls – also known as Tibetan or Nepalese singing bowls – and the special sounds they make, called sound massage. The author discusses the meeting between East and West, singing bowls, sacrificial dishes, how the bowls work, synchronization and inner massage, shamanism and brain waves, and practical instruction for working with these sounds. Although the short scope of this book won't provice absolute answers to all the questions you may have about the bowls, it does provice practical information about using them, as well as showing you how to go about finding the bowl that is right for you. The mysteries explained here are a wonderful overview if you want to open your heart and mind to the therapeutic value of this phenomenon. Illustrated. 110 pp.

ISBN 90-74597-01-7

Eva Rudy Jansen

The Book of Buddhas
Ritual Symbolism Used on Buddhist Statuary and Ritual Objects

In Buddhism, every symbol has a meaning, and this book explores the symbolism of the ritual objects that are used on statues and in paintings, and explains the ritual meaning of the objects associated with Buddhism. This book is not a comprehensive and exhaustive study, but serves as an introduction for Western students to Buddhism itself. The author examines the Three Mysteries, mudras, asanas, Manushri Buddhas, Transcendental Buddhas, Adibuddha, Tara, Majushri, and Avalokiteshvara. Also discussed is Yidams, Gods and Goddesses, dakinis and goinis, and the Laughing Buddha. Each individual symbol is clearly depicted and accompanied by a short explanation of its significance. Includes an index for easy reference. Illustrated. 126 pp.

ISBN 90-74597-02-5

Eva Rudy Jansen

The Book of Hindu Imagery
The Gods and their Symbols

Hinduism is more than a religion; it is a way of life that has developed over approximately 5 millennia. Its rich history has made the structure of its mythical and philosophical principles into a highly differentiated maze, of which total knowledge is a practical impossibility. This volume cannot offer a complete survey of the meaning of Hinduism, but is does provice an extensive compilation of important deities and their divine manifestations, so that modern students can understand the Hindu pantheon. To facilitate easy recognition, a survey of ritual gestures, postures, attires and attributes, and an index are included. Over 100 illustrations and several photographs. 158 pp.

ISBN 90-74597-07-6 PBK
ISBN 90-74597-10-6 CLOTH

Dirk Schellberg

Didgeridoo
Ritual Origins and Playing Techniques

The didgeridoo plays an important role in the creation myths of the Australian Aborigines. The deep sound of this wind instrument helped create the world. This book describes the origins of the didgeridoo, the stories about the instrument and the players. It not only deals with Australian musicians and band, but also discusses how Western therapists have discovered new applications for this ancient sound. Also shows how to build an instrument, or what to look for in purchasing one. Illustrated. Appendix includes a reading list and discography. 158 pp.

ISBN 90-74597-13-0

George Hulskramer

The Life of Buddha
From Prince Siddhartha to Buddha

There are few histories of Prince Siddhartha that are as accessible to all ages as this one. In comic-book format, Hulskramer tells the colorful story of the Buddha Siddhartha, skillfully illustrated by Nepalese artists Raju Babu Shakya and Bijay Raj Shakya. This is a readable biography for anyone who is intrested in Buddhism, a wonderful, exotic fairy for lovers of beautiful illustrated stories, and a collector's item for cartoon enthusiasts. 72 pp.

ISBN 90-74597-17-3

Töm Klöwer

The Joy of Drumming

Drums en Percussion Instruments from around the World

If you think you're not musical, think again! Rhythm, the foundation of music, is all around and within us. In the womb, we began our experience of the world through the sounds of our mother's hearbeat and the cadence of her voice. Experiencing rhythm and movement is an essential part of healthy living, and Töm Klöwer shows you how to reconnect with this life-affirming energy. Within these pages you're sure to find at least one instrument that will get you resonating, and once you do, you can work with the simple rhythm exercises Klöwer presents to begin your journey into the world of drumming. The book includes over *100 illustrations of different drums, gongs, and sound effect instruments,* along with descriptions of how they are made, and basic playing techniques. From the most ancient instruments to the most modern inventions, from *Asia, Australia, Africa, and South America,* one of these instruments is sure to capture your imagination.

For more advanced drummers, Klöwer presents traditional rhythm patterns from Africa and South America, and music therapists will be inspired by the broad range of instruments he describes. His exercises can be performed by an individuel as well as a group of people.

This book is an appeal for a rediscovery of the spiritual and physical healing potential of rhythmic sound, and for the importance of musical creativity in our daily lives. Klöwer discusses how different cultures from around the world have used percussion in their spiritual practices for healing and conflict resolution, in communication, and for maintaining a sense of freedom and integrity. Everyone is creative and has musical potential begin your fulfilling journey with this book.

ISBN 90-74597-13-9

Your Own Memorandum
of Fun and Progress

In working with the health balls, you will certainly invent your own ways of playing and exercising with them. You will probably also note differences, even improvement, in the condition of your body and mind.

It might be a good idea to keep track of these improvements and, above all, to write down your own special discoveries and ways of working with the balls.

On the next pages you can make a start with your own exclusive exercisebook and health diary.

May pleasure be your steady companion!

Health Diary

Health Diary